This book belongs to:

_____

This book is dedicated to Casper and my wonderful family.

Dreams can become a reality, and asking for help is okay.

First published in 2023
Text and illustrations copyright © Sarah Halley
All rights reserved
No part of this publication may be produced or transmitted in any form or by any means, electronic, photocopying, recording or otherwise, without the publisher's written permission.

ISBN: 978-1-7395356-0-5 PB
ISBN: 978-1-7395356-1-2 HB

The Storm Inside

Sarah Halley

Billy loves to read;
he reads every day.
He would spend his days with books in his hand,
exploring new worlds and learning new things.

Billy loved to read more than anything in the world, but he didn't love to tidy up. He would often leave his books scattered around the room. But it was finally time to tidy up.

Billy thought carrying all of his books at once would be quicker.

Billy needed to investigate; he noticed a scratch on the floor. He felt terrible!

Maybe if he just ignored it, he thought it would go away on its own.

As Billy lay in bed that night, he tossed and turned. His mind rumbled about the scratch on the floor. He dreamt that the scratch grew bigger and bigger!

Billy didn't feel like breakfast; All he could think about was the scratch on the floor.

Billy tried to distract himself, but he couldn't shake the thought of it. He began to feel sad. But the sound of the storm outside felt like it was getting closer and closer. He decided to run home before the storm arrived.

But wait, what's this? A storm cloud was inside his house; it must have been lost!

But the more Billy watched, the bigger the storm cloud grew.

(Maybe he could hide from it?)

Billy used his best disguise!
(no one would recognise him)
But it was still there!

Hiding didn't work; it only grew bigger; maybe he could run away from it?
(Billy was the fastest in his class)

Hmmm, running away didn't work either. The cloud began to rumble, louder and louder. Billy decided to ignore it.

(It would disappear in no time)

But it didn't...

Busy thinking about the scratch on the floor, Billy hadn't noticed the cloud grow into a ginormous storm!

It grew larger and larger, filling the whole room!

Billy didn't know what to do; the storm was taking over.

Billy couldn't ignore the storm anymore; he couldn't control it.
Until...

Billy remembered just what to do.

Billy closed his eyes and took a big breath in; he knew exactly what to do!

Billy remembered what his sister had said,

"No worries too big,

no worries too small,

take a deep breath in,

to calm them all."

Billy decided to tell his sister all about the floor and the storm. They spoke for hours and wiped away his tears. To his surprise, he slowly felt the storm grow smaller.

From that day on, he didn't ignore his worries. He knew he didn't have to face them alone.

www.ingramcontent.com/pod-product-compliance
Lightning Source LLC
Chambersburg PA
CBRC091454160426
43209CB00024B/1891